WHEN THE SPIRIT MOVES YOU

Bb TENOR SAXOPHONE/TRUMPET

Eb ALTO SAXOPHONE

To access audio visit:
www.halleonard.com/mylibrary

Enter Code
3108-1276-9641-4763

ISBN 978-1-59615-687-6

EXCLUSIVELY DISTRIBUTED BY

HAL•LEONARD®

7777 W. BLUEMOUND RD. P.O. BOX 13819 MILWAUKEE, WI 53213

Visit Hal Leonard Online at
www.halleonard.com

Boots Randolph

When Boots Randolph starts "tootin' his horn," he does more than just play the saxophone. More than just pop out music notes. And that's why his saxophone sounds like it can sing, can talk, can almost speak to deaf ears! His ability is awesome. His versatile style has no equal. And he's been bringing audiences to their feet ever since the early sixties, when his signature song, *Yakety Sax*, first hit the airwaves. It took off like gangbusters and turned the young musician into a celebrity, probably before some of his friends in the hills of Kentucky could have even spelled it!

A native of Paducah, Kentucky, Boots, whose real name is Homer Louis Randolph, grew up in the rural community of Cadiz. Young Homer was tagged with the nickname "Boots" by his brother, Bob, without dreaming it would one day be that of an International Star! The Randolphs were always a creative clan, rich in musical talent, and their family band initially provided Boots with the first of his opportunities on stage. He learned to play a variety of instruments, but settled on the sax at age 16. Years later, he was to make it his career choice while working for Uncle Sam, during which time he was privileged to perform with the Army band. After his discharge in 1946, Boots Randolph began putting his "chops" to work professionally. However, it wasn't until 1961 that he moved to Music City, on the heels of his successful trademark tune or, as he tells it, "that song (*Yakety Sax*) is what took me out of the hills of Kentucky and put me in the hills of Tennessee!" The song gave him the prestige of being a hit artist. Almost instantly, the Sax Man was seriously being sought after as a studio musician, and he was soon picking saxophone on recording sessions for numerous stars.

Boots Randolph was the first to ever play sax on recordings with Elvis, and the only one to ever play solo with him, in addition to recording on the soundtracks for eight of his movies. Boots also played on such diverse recordings as Roy Orbison's *Oh, Pretty Woman*, Al Hirt's *Java*, REO Speedwagon's *Little Queenie*, and Brenda Lee's *Rockin' 'Round the Christmas Tree*. In fact, he has a 30-year history of playing on records with her, including *I Want to Be Wanted* and *I'm Sorry*. An array of other artists who have added the Yakety Sax touch to their recordings include Chet Atkins, Buddy Holly, Floyd Cramer, Alabama, Johnny Cash, Richie Cole, Pete Fountain, Tommy Newsom and Doc Severinsen.

His unique style of sax coupled with tremendous popularity on Music City sessions in the sixties, automatically made Randolph a major player in creating the now famous "Nashville Sound." Without question, it was Randolph's particular blend of Dixieland jazz, along with some swingin' honky-tonk, which helped Nashville music makers turn hillbilly records into a hybrid sound that literally transformed Nashville into the Country Music Capitol of the world! And to this day, Randolph still has more calls for his "saxy" sound at studio sessions than he can handle. While most people only associate Randolph with his self-written, multi-million seller *Yakety Sax*, he also had other big hits in the form of gold (a half-million in sales) on *The Shadow of Your Smile* in 1966. Plus, he "hit gold" numerous other times through recordings made with others, including *Honey in the Horn*, *Java*, and *Cotton* by Al Hirt, not to mention the countless consecutive Gold records by Elvis. He also has over 40 albums to his credit on the Monument label. Randolph spent 15 years touring with fellow instrumentalists Chet Atkins and Floyd Cramer. He's also taken his "Yakety Sax" to numerous network TV shows including the *Ed Sullivan Show*, *Kraft Music Hall*, *The Tonight Show* with Johnny Carson, *Merv Griffin Show*, *Mike Douglas Show*, *Joey Bishop Show*, *Steve Lawrence Show*, and the Boston Pops. He's made numerous TV appearances on TNN's *Music City Tonight* and *Prime Time Country*.

After performing all across the country in some of the most posh clubs ever built, Boots Randolph took the plunge in 1977, borrowed half-a-million bucks to restore an historic building in Nashville Printer's Alley, and opened his own dinner club called Boots Randolph's. He performed there on a regular basis, and enjoyed a successful run with the club for 17 years, before he called it quits. When he closed the club, Randolph had vowed to "go fishing," but it was barely a year later in 1996, when he found himself back in business, pairing up with Danny Davis, as they embarked on a brand new venture in Nashville called The Stardust Theatre, featuring both artists in concert. Two years later, they each returned to their respective on-the-road schedules. Having headlined at almost every fair, jazz festival and convention in the country, as well as performing throughout Europe, definitely puts Boots Randolph in the category of being a saxophone player WITH EXPERIENCE!

Over the years, this legendary musician has written chapter after chapter of music history, forever etched in sound and to this day, he continues to entertain audiences with the same enthusiasm he's had since day one. Boots is his name. SAX is his game! His horn is a Selmer Super 80 Series II. He uses a Bobby Dukoff D-9 mouthpiece, and a #3 Rico reed.

Music Minus One is particularly pleased to be able to add Boots Randolph to the MMO family of fine musicians who have graced our catalogue. This illustrious saxophonist, so intimately associated with country music, has performed with every notable singer of that genre, Elvis, Orbison, Chet Atkins, Buddy Holly, Floyd Cramer, Johnny Cash, Alabama, the list seems endless. His pop music credentials include Brenda Lee, Al Hirt, Richie Cole, Pete Fountain, Tommy Newsom, Doc Severinsen; his greatness has touched greatness.

CONTENTS

Bb Instrument

Just a Closer Walk with Thee

Anonymous
arr. by Tim Smith

One measure of taps (4 taps) precedes music

Tenor Sax
(or Bb Trumpet)

B♭ Instrument

In the Garden

Traditional
arr. by Tim Smith

Tenor Sax
(or B♭ Trumpet)

B♭ Instrument

The Lord's Prayer

Traditional
arr. by Tim Smith

The Old Rugged Cross

Traditional
arr. by Tim Smith

**Tenor Sax
(or B♭ Trumpet)**

Bb Instrument

Medley:
Shall We Gather at the River/When the Roll Is Called Up Yonder
In the Sweet Bye and Bye

Traditional
arr. by Tim Smith

Tenor Sax
(or Bb Trumpet)

B♭ Instrument

What a Friend We Have in Jesus

Traditional
arr. by Tim Smith

Tenor Sax
(or B♭ Trumpet)

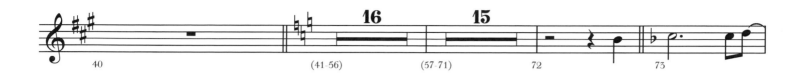

Patriotic Medley:
America the Beautiful/God Bless America/When the Saints Go Marching In

B♭ Instrument

Amazing Grace

Traditional
arr. by Tim Smith

Tenor Sax
(or B♭ Trumpet)

Bb Instrument

Precious Lord, Take My Hand

Thomas Dorsey/George Allen

Give Me That Old Time Religion/Will the Circle Be Unbroken

Traditional
arr. by Tim Smith

Eb Instrument

Just a Closer Walk with Thee

Anonymous
arr. by Tim Smith

One measure of taps (4 taps) precedes music

Eb Alto Sax

Eb Instrument

In the Garden

Traditional
arr. by Tim Smith

The Lord's Prayer

Traditional
arr. by Tim Smith

E♭ Instrument

The Old Rugged Cross

Traditional
arr. by Tim Smith

E♭ Alto Sax

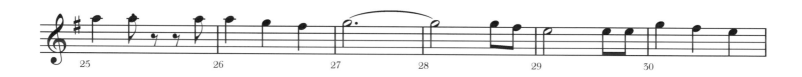

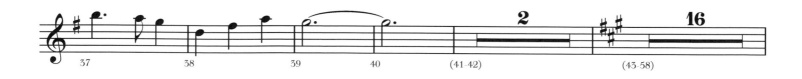

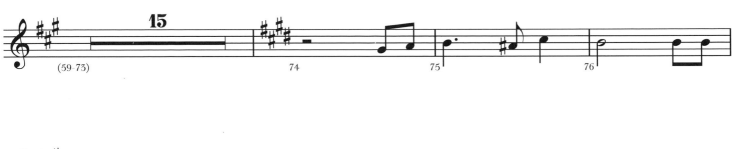

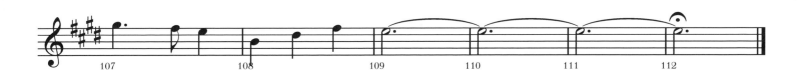

Eb Instrument

Medley:
Shall We Gather at the River/When the Roll Is Called Up Yonder
In the Sweet Bye and Bye

Traditional
arr. by Tim Smith

Eb Instrument

What a Friend We Have in Jesus

Traditional
arr. by Tim Smith

E♭ Alto Sax

E♭ Instrument

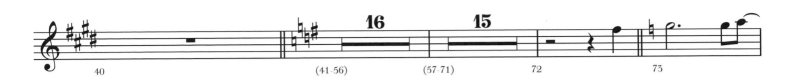

Patriotic Medley:
America the Beautiful/God Bless America/When the Saints Go Marching In

Traditional
arr. by Tim Smith

E♭ Instrument

Amazing Grace

Traditional
arr. by Tim Smith

Eb Instrument

Precious Lord, Take My Hand

Thomas Dorsey/George Allen

Eb Instrument

Give Me That Old Time Religion/Will the Circle Be Unbroken

Traditional
arr. by Tim Smith

Eb Instrument

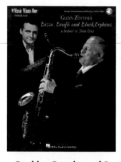

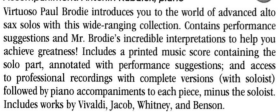